Only God

Going Forward with Jesus through Life's Experiences

Howard "Buddy" Dunn

Parson's Porch Books

Only God: Going Forward with Jesus through Life's Experiences

ISBN: Softcover 978-1-955581-63-9

Parson's Porch Books is an imprint of Parson's Porch *&* Company (PP*&*C) in Cleveland, Tennessee. PP*&*C is an innovative organization which raises money by publishing books of noted authors, representing all genres. Its face and voice is **David Russell Tullock** (dtullock@parsonsporch.com).

Parson's Porch *&* Company *turns books into bread & milk* by sharing its profits with the poor.

www.parsonsporch.com

Only God

Contents

Dedication 7

Acknowledgments 9

Foreword 11

Preface..13

The First Vision and a Promise...15

My Plans and God's Plan 16

Saved from Revenge 17

"Buddy You Didn't Do It – I Did"..20

The Big Oak Dream...22

Like Lifting a Child 24

It Should Have Been Impossible 25

"I Don't Know How You're Going To Do It" 26

I Had Two Minutes Left 27

Tomorrow, About 4:30 PM..28

It's Going To Stop 29

"Can You Stop The Rain?"...30

"Lord, It's Okay If I Get Wet" 31

I Hope You See The Selfishness...32

"I Would Like to See a Streak Of Lightning"............................33

"Stormy Wind Fulfilling His Word" (Psalm 148:8) 35

The Great Judgment of God..37

It Must Have Started Right Over My Tent 39

A Vision Of Angels...40

The Mountain Of Blessing..41

"I Climbed up the Mountain with Jesus" 42

Obedience to the Father is Never a Small Thing.......................43

Lord, Give Her My Blessing..44

Double Portion 46

The Father's Touch..47

Relationship or Fellowship?..50

"My Word, Driven by my Spirit"...51

Hanging by a Thread...53

"Thanks for Spending Time with Me" 55

"Old Men will Dream Dreams"..57

Whether by Whirlwind or Wheelchair 60

During a Prayer Ride...62

Look into my Eyes… I Began To Feel His Aloneness.....................63
Almost, but Lost!...64
"Remember Lot's wife"...66
A Body Slain and a Soul Saved...67
Prayer for a Stranger, Who Turned Out to be a Neighbor 68
Not Good Enough..70
A Shaking Finger, a Stronger Friendship.......................................72
Released by Satan, Received into Glory..73
Pretending to be Asleep, but Listening..74
Jesus Never Fails 75
Not Expected to Live through the Night..77
"Nothing Short of a Miracle!"...78
When a 3-Year-Old Wants Prayer..79
126 Years Old and Running 35 Mph 80
Even a Goldfish Matters to God!...81
Just Walk Across...82
Just Follow..83
Instead, He Gave Me Wisdom...84
"Just Go Forward"...85
"There's No Way!"...86
"I Saw It!"...87
Calming the Inner Storm...88
Recovered from the Gates of Hell! 89
Mistaken for an Angel! 90
The Fireball Was As Big As My Head 92
I Heard a Crackling Sound..93
270,000 Volts! 94
Preserved Yet Again...95
Seeing our Father through our Work..96
Lay Hands on it 97
Start the car!...98
The Living God Sees All Things...99
My Prayer for You... 101

Dedication

This book is dedicated to the many people who, over the years, told me, "You should write a book."

Acknowledgments

I want to thank Lauren Leigh Powell for helping to type the original manuscript from my handwritten copy.

Also, I am grateful to Edward N. Gross, who kept things going on track with his technical and navigational ability, and who connected me with David Russell Tullock, the kind owner of Parsons Porch Publishing.

Finally, and especially, I acknowledge our Lord Jesus, who had the main part in every story. Without Him none of it would have even happened.

Foreword

My wife, Debby, and I are now serving as missionaries to the Delmarva Peninsula. Our calling is to help both Christians and non-Christians become disciples of Jesus Christ. Disciples who know how to follow Jesus and MULTIPLY by leading others to do the same. We are blessed to serve with Compassion for Life (see www.compassionforlife.org). We are focusing on the 14 counties of the Eastern Shores of Delaware, Maryland and Virginia. And prayerfully laboring to see a Disciple Making Movement (DMM) in each of these counties.

In following this call of God, I entered Caroline County in Maryland. As I connected with real people of prayer, I met Buddy Dunn. As we would meet and pray, he would just tell me a story of God's leading him and using him. I knew that unless I "kept in step with the Spirit," like Buddy did, I could never help many Christians who merely "go to church." Like many others before me, I told him that he should write some of these stories down so that they are not lost. He is now 77 years old.

God used Buddy's stories (not his preaching, which I have never heard), to help lead me to a life that is much more surrendered to Jesus and filled with the Holy Spirit. I hope and pray that brushing up alongside of Buddy, as you read the following stories, will do the same for you. Buddy told me that his goal in sharing was that he just wanted others to know the Lord and enjoy His presence and power, too.

I would have sub-titled this book: The Amazing Life and Work of Buddy Dunn. But that was too self-promoting for Buddy, who truly wants all glory to be given to His Lord and Savior Jesus Christ.

Dr. Edward N Gross

Christmas 2021

Preface

I was born at Lincoln University, in Chester County Pennsylvania, on Oct. 22, 1944. My father was from Johnson County in Tennessee. My mother, from Buchanan County in Virginia. Both my grandmothers were of Native American ancestry. My 5th and 7th generation ancestors were Cherokee chiefs. We started moving South in 1946. The first stop was near Rising Sun, MD, near Cecilton, Maryland.

In 1948 we moved to the Federalsburg area. I started school in 1950 at Federalsburg, Maryland. We lived on a dairy farm between Harmony and American Corner. I have told many people that I had the best upbringing anyone could have.

We were taught, (I was the third of four boys), to get up in the morning before daylight and go to work. We learned to do what we were told, when we were told, and the way we were told to do it. When my two older brothers went into the military, they wrote home that they got to lay in bed until 5:30 AM, and that they already knew how to take orders.

In 1953, my youngest brother died. Good friends, family and faith got us through that time. My mother called us in, put our heads in her lap and said, "Boys, you don't have a little brother anymore." He wasn't with us; but he never really left us. The circle is unbroken, and someday we will see him again.

In 1955, we had another brother. He left us in 1966 just weeks short of his 11th birthday. Again friends, family, but especially faith carried us through. The more heartbreak that happened, the stronger became our faith. This was not belief in a god; but, in the one and only true God that knows all there is from the beginning.

In 1958, my hip came out of place, and I walked nearly a year with it out. The day I went to the hospital in Easton MD, I was on a hay wagon behind a baler loading the wagon. My mother picked me up and we went to see a doctor at the hospital. He took hold of my leg moved it and said, "Can he stay?" The rest of that story has already been written. The living God knew everything about me, He planned my way. Even when I went astray, He was there to bring me back. He knows the way to take, as you will see in the following stories.

I went to work in the Fall of 1961 at the local bakery. I worked 90 to 100 hours a week while still being in school. I started off cleaning floors and was plant Superintendent when I left 11 years later. I then started operating heavy equipment in 1972 and did so until 2000. Except for the first company I worked for, I was the job supervisor as well as an operator. The Lord always promoted me to higher positions with more responsibility. I hope you will see through some of my life-stories, that our greatest promotion is leading someone to higher ground in Christ.

I've been the pastor of Faith Fellowship Church near Preston, MD, since 1985 when the pastor died, and I was asked to fill in until they found a pastor. It's now been over 35 years!

Buddy Dunn

December 2021

The First Vision and a Promise

Around **1957** I was standing at the center entrance to the feeding shed, looking out toward the "loafing shed". I could see a few cows, the barnyard and the shed. Then the scene changed, and I saw the hall of what looked like a hospital. I was on a gurney being pushed down the hall, then it was gone. I had this vision when I was 13. It was not a dream in my mind; but a vision I saw with my eyes.

In **1959** I was put in the Children's Hospital in Baltimore. My hip had come out of place about a year earlier and we were told it was sprained. I was operated on and was in a body cast for 3 months. I could see 3 toes on my right foot and from the knee down on the left leg. The cast came to the upper portion of my chest. I was about 2 months in the cast when I saw another boy a little older than I dragging both feet as he walked on his crutches. His operation didn't work.

As I thought about the future and my plans for it, I had only one hope. I had already, before going to the hospital, made a profession of faith in Jesus. So, I prayed, "Lord, if you'll let me walk again, I'll serve you." It was another month after I got out of the cast learning to move my leg, but it was months later before I could put weight on my leg. Finally, I was able to walk again.

My Plans and God's Plan

I had made a rash statement in a time of frustration and anger at the end of the summer of 1958, that I would never pick any more tomatoes, peppers or cucumbers. I spent from the second week of June until the 21st of October **1959** in the hospital. I was rarely taken out of my room because it took 4 people to put me on a stretcher. I never saw the sunshine for about 10 weeks.

I saw kids that had been born without hands, arms, or legs. One had parts of his arms and legs burned off in a fire. Some were hooked to tubes and would never be able to leave the hospital.

My right leg was smaller and weaker than my left, 3/4" to 1" shorter also. I was told no running, no physical contact sports, no heavy lifting, no Phys. Ed. My plans had changed, but God's plan was at work.

Saved from Revenge

In the summer of **1960,** I was on light duty and one day I had been dropped off at Nagel's Pond to swim. A friend was to meet me there, and I anticipated having a good time swimming and talking with my friend. It would have been just the two of us guys. It had been only a few minutes when someone else came to swim. They were a few years older, had their driver's license and was driving a car. They also captivated the attention of my friend, and I was on the outside of the activities and conversation.

Again, I made a rash statement that came of envy, jealously and pride. That ended in me taking a sucker punch to the stomach, picking up my towel and walking home, too embarrassed to tell anyone what had happened. I don't remember going swimming anymore that summer.

I didn't know the boy's name but remembered his face. Bitterness filled me, and I would dream of the next meeting we would have and how different the outcome would be. The work that I did, building my muscles and, in a few years, I would let others hit me in the stomach just to see the look on their faces when it didn't bother me. I could arm curl 110 lbs. with one arm and do one handed push-ups as fast as most could do with two hands.

Many times, my thoughts would go to the next time this nameless boy and I met. I lived the event in my mind many times. Along with the strength, my hands became so calloused I would push thumb tacks in the palms of my hands and never feel it. To show off, I would snuff out cigars in the palm of my hand with no sign of a burn. I would catch the pans coming

17

out of a 476-degree oven and put them on a rack. My knuckles were knotted with callouses from the type of work I was doing. I would hold glass jars in one hand and punch them with the other and shatter them.

I would envision crushing this person at our next encountered, I really believed someday it would come and the victory and revenge would be mine and sweet. Bitterness and anger had not only hardened my inside. I looked considerably older than I was. My face reflected the hate I had inside.

The day finally came when the nameless man and I met. The company I worked for had gone to night work and I wasn't able to sleep during the daytime. I had been awake all-day Sunday, Sunday night, Monday, Monday night and Tuesday morning. Just after sunrise, on my way home, I turned off one road onto another. I was very sleepy and pushed the side ventilator open to get some air in my face. I was about a mile and a half from home.

As I opened the vent, I stepped on the gas to resume my speed, I felt the pickup shake. It was like a cloud lifted from my eyes, my mind had kept seeing my progress at one speed, when actually I had greatly increased my speed and had come to the curve in the road and was starting down into the ditch and then into the woods. The bumper of the airborne pickup hit a tree seven feet up and uprooted the tree. My arm was still outside the pickup and was between the door and ground. When I landed, the ventilator cut my wrist right between my leather glove and leather jacket. The tendons to three fingers, the nerves, blood vessels and arteries were completely severed.

I saw blood everywhere in the pickup, but I didn't know where I was bleeding at the time. I brought my arm into open the door and saw what had happened. I applied pressure to the wrist to stop the bleeding and climbed out the window. I started toward the closest house when I saw someone running toward me pulling their T-shirt off to wrap around my wrist.

I recognized the face of the one who several years before had sucker punched me and I had prepared myself to crush when I saw him again. He ran and got his car and took me home. My dad took me to the hospital. They said at the hospital that I didn't have enough blood left to be conscious.

I had bled on the cloth seat of the man's car, blood was on the floorboards, and his shirt was covered with my blood.

By the time I got out of the hospital and was able to get around, the man had moved, and no one knew where. The incident happened April 4th, **1963**. I say incident because it was no accident, it was a part of God's plan. He showed me the results of envy, jealousy, bitterness, anger and pride. I later began to call these incidents: love letters from my Father.

It was many years later when I met the man again. He had moved to Salisbury and began going to church and had accepted Jesus as his Savior. By this time, I too had rededicated my life to Jesus and was in church whenever the doors were open. This was all in God's great plan of redemption for me.

"Buddy You Didn't Do It – I Did"

In the summer of **1964**, I received a call at work saying that my girlfriend had been swimming, and someone had jumped on her and she was at the Dr's office. I found out she almost drowned, she had been knocked out and someone saw it happen and responded quickly enough to save her.

I was still filled with anger at this time. I left work and went to the doctor's office. The bleeding had stopped, but she was still in shock, trembling. I carried her home which was about 10 miles out of town. After seeing she was alright, my mind went to revenge and the person who did it would pay. I should have been grateful she was alive and alright and sought out the person who saved her life and thanked them, but I didn't.

I left her place with the intent to inflict as much pain on the person as possible before killing him. Anger and bitterness were so powerful I thought nothing of the overall outcome of me killing someone regardless of how justified I felt it was.

As I drove back towards the lake, visions of how I would do it filled my mind so much so that I wasn't paying any attention to my driving. I came to an S-turn in the road, the car speed had maxed out and was going far too fast to make the turn. There was an embankment, then trees ending in a stream at the bottom. My thought was to take it head on and hope the seat belt helps somehow. At the last instant the wheel turned to the left, the car went sideways, then straightened up and crossed a narrow bridge, then sideways the other way, then straightened up in the road. It had not hit either shoulder of the road.

I was in wonder, then heard the wind blowing in the car. Looking over my shoulder I saw the rear passenger side glass was halfway down, all the windows were up when I entered the turn, then I heard a voice out loud say, *"Buddy, you didn't do it, I did."* I was a hot-rodder and drove hard, I knew the car could not make the turn. I was going too fast and had completely powered out, I had nothing to prevent what should have happened.

I finished the ride to town at a slower pace with thought of what had happened and what I had heard as clear as if someone was sitting next to me in the car.

As I was going through town on my way to the lake a former classmate flagged me down. I stopped and had gotten out by the time he had gotten to me. He first asked if Susie was alright, then told me he had been the one to hit her. He said he had jumped and while he was in the air she came up from under the water and it was too late to do anything. Then he said, "You can kill me if you want to, I'm sorry, I would never have done it on purpose."

Having known the man for years, I knew he wouldn't. It was clearly an accident, but Satan was using my mind, energy and strength to destroy myself. The Heavenly Father didn't allow it to happen. My girlfriend became my wife in **1965** and at the time of this writing we've been married 56 years.

I was filled with anger, hatred, rage with nothing but killing on my mind. God had no reason to prevent my death, except for His mercy and grace. Still, it was several years before I began to serve Him.

The Big Oak Dream

As the years went by, I kept getting farther away from a life that showed any form of Christianity. I hated many things I was doing, even cried at night saying, "God, I don't want to do these things," then turn around and do them again.

One night in the early part of **1972** I had a dream that seemed so real it woke me up.

I was walking in the yard and came to a big oak tree. The roots were raised out of the ground at the base of the tree and two of the bigger ones were like a V coming away from the tree. As I looked at these roots I saw a pool of water between the roots, and in the pool of water was my oldest daughter, only she was an infant in the dream.

She was lying seemingly in about two to three inches of water. I said "Honey, what are you doing there?" and I bent down to lift her out. As I bent down, she went deeper into the water, then I was on my knees, and she had gone under the water. I fell flat on the ground with my face pressed hard against the root with my arm extended as far as I could into the water and I was waving it frantically and could not touch her, nor the sides or bottom of the hole.

In panic I screamed, "Oh God, please help me!" At that instant the heel of her foot hit the palm of my hand and I grabbed it and pulled her out. Then I awoke. For several months that dream would come to my mind, and I would relive the same anxiousness over and over again. One day as I was mowing the grass the dream came again as fresh as ever. I stopped pushing the mower and asked, "God, what does this dream mean?" The answer came clear and unhesitatingly, *"If you don't call on me, I'm going to take your daughter."* Many other things had happened, setbacks we call them, but this got my attention, and it wasn't long before I changed jobs and we went to church, and I rededicated my life to Jesus. The love of God goes beyond anything we can understand.

Like Lifting a Child

Many things have happened over the years to let me know that we do have a guide, and I cannot help but believe that God the Father, Himself, is that guide.

Once a couple of years after I left my other jobs, I had begun running a dragline, a piece of heavy equipment used for digging ponds and dragging ditches, I was working in a lot of mud, I was digging drainage ditched for the Soil Conservation District. The brakes on the machine needed to be adjusted and as I was walking around the machine on the counterweight, it felt like someone put both hands on my back and pushed very hard. I had stopped the machine with the back toward the ditch, the bottom of the ditch was at least 10 feet down. As I went off the machine it was so fast my head was lower than my feet which was still on the counterweight, and I felt a pressure under my armpits as if someone had taken hold of me like we would lift a child. My upper body stopped falling and my feet swung down under me. I was expecting a jolt when my feet hit the ground but there was none, I was completely on balance, I knew the hands either of an angel or my Father, Himself, had set me down safely.

It Should Have Been Impossible

The Lord anointed me to operate the different kinds of equipment I had to use. I could feel a warmth come over me and it was as if the machine operated itself. At times I was asked to do things the machine should not have been able to do; but the job was done anyway.

Once my boss told me to dig a channel from the river to the property owner's pier. It was on a curve in the river and had silted in so much the pier couldn't be used. The owner walked out on the silt to show me where he wanted the channel and was sinking several inches each step he took. I walked the excavator over 150 feet over river silt and dug the channel as I came back in. It should have been impossible to have walked a twenty-two-ton machine across nothing but rotting vegetation.

"I Don't Know How You're Going To Do It"

I was asked by my boss to do a job concerning which he said, "I am asking you to do a job with a backhoe that needs to be done with an excavator and I don't know how you're going to do it." In about 3 ½ hours I had radioed the boss and told him I was ready for stone to be delivered. He said he had to see this and came to the job site. He said he thought it would take at least a day and half to clear the area and shape the ground for stone.

I could tell many, many times of my Father's anointing the work of my hands and at another time I may write them down, even if just to refresh my gratefulness to my heavenly Father for His blessing on my work.

I Had Two Minutes Left

There have been many times when things have happened concerning the weather. it may not have been the first answer to a request concerning rain, but it is my first recollection of an answer.

It was the early to mid-**1970's** and I had been working a lot and had not had time to cultivate the garden. On the way home the sky darkened as if it would rain, which if it did, I would not be able to cultivate. My request was, "Father, I need half an hour to cultivate the garden, that's all." The clouds blew away, the sky cleared. When I got home Mom was pulling weeds from her garden. I went straight to the tractor and started cultivating, not even stopping to speak. I finished and put the tractor up, then looked at my watch. I had two minutes left of the half hour I had asked for. I told Mom she had better head for the house because it was going to start raining in about two minutes. She looked around and said, "It didn't look like rain." I told her again if she didn't start now, she would get wet. Before she got to the house it was pouring rain, she got soaked and it was just half an hour from the time I started the tractor to begin working the garden.

Tomorrow, About 4:30 PM

Another time I was asked to take prayer request at a church evening service. A Mr. Tull asked to pray for rain. Right away I asked how much and when do you want it? His answer was: two inches and as soon as we can get it. My answer was tomorrow about 4:30 pm it will begin to rain. It was several weeks before I went back to that church but when I did Mr. Tull saw me coming and waited outside for me. He said he couldn't wait to tell me, it started raining right when I said, and he had two inches in his rain gauge when it stopped. I had said what I said because I felt the Father's permission to ask what I will.

It's Going To Stop

Another time, at my Dad's place, I was working on my pickup truck and had the hood up. My Dad and a couple of others were in the garage talking and watching e when a very dark cloud came over and it started to rain really hard. We had a metal roof on the garage and could hardly hear each other except to talk really loudly.

My Dad said my truck wasn't going to start after the rain. I asked why? He said I left the hood up and water was running down on the distributor. I said, "I'll close it." He said I would get wet if I went out now. I said, "No I wouldn't." He said, "Why not?" I had started toward the door, when I answered, "Because it's going to stop."

The instant I said stop, it stopped, my foot would have been in the rain had it not stopped when it did. I continued to the truck and closed the hood, when I turned around all three were staring at me with their mouths wide open. It was as if someone just turned a ball valve and the water stopped immediately. I didn't have a drop on me. Again, something inside said speak it.

"Can You Stop The Rain?"

I was on a job at Horns Point digging a trench while men were installing drainage pipe for their fishponds. The pipes were 9 to 10 feet in the ground. A heavy, dark cloud came over, the wind began to blow, and it started to rain a little. The job supervisor came over to me and said, "If it rains, we will have to dig everything up and start over." Then he asked, "Can you stop the rain?" To ask such a question after knowing me for two days, I believed he had been prompted by the Father to ask it. I answered, "No, but I know the one who can." I took my hat off, stuck my head out the door of the machine and said, "Thank you Father for hearing me." And put my hat back on. The rain stopped immediately, the clouds cleared, and I began thanking my Father for it. We finished the job. The weatherman was calling for severe storms that afternoon, but the Creator, who puts all things in order, reserves the right to change anything He wants.

"Lord, It's Okay If I Get Wet"

One afternoon I had finished work, clouds had gathered, and it was starting to rain, the wind was picking up also. I had a distance to go to get to my truck and then had to gas my truck up for the next day. I said "Lord, I really don't want to get wet." It stopped raining and I again, thanked my Father. I got in my truck, drove to the gas pumps and went inside the office to get a gas ticket. As I walked to the office, I began thinking of how dry it was and how the farmers needed rain and thought how selfish it was because I didn't want to get wet. I had entered the office, had gotten the ticket and as I turned to leave, I said "Lord, it's okay if I get wet." Just as I pushed the door open lightning hit very close, the bottom fell out and men ran as fast as they could for the building. I again saw my Father at work. How could I not continue on as if it was not raining, after all, I said it was okay to get wet. I sang as I filled the tank, I had to put a piece of cardboard over the filler tube to keep the water out. The other men were standing in one of the bay doors calling me crazy, telling me it's raining, get out of the rain. I could only rejoice and experiencing yet another answer to prayer.

I Hope You See The Selfishness

I have many other stories about the rain I could tell but I am only going to relate one more. In **1979** I changed jobs and began again to do drainage work with a private contractor for soil conservation.

The first job wasn't far from home, but about an hour and a half from the company's office. I would be in charge and, of course, wanted to make a good showing. The job was very wet, water was standing in the fields which makes things more difficult.

I said, "Father, please hold the rain so we can finish this job in record time." I hope you see the selfishness of my request, I wanted to look good for the new boss. We had a winter drought that year. We had some rain and snow but was not enough to stop the work. One of the farmers said he had been tilling that area for 17 years and had never seen it so dry; where his pickup was sitting was usually under a foot and a half of water.

We finished the job in excellent time, made the boss money and I looked good. Then I began to think, because of the Winter drought, the water table was down, the winter grain had not grown as it should, and Spring planting would be slow starting.

I decided my Father knew more about the weather, what was needed and when, than I did. I asked that it begin to rain in divine order and have not asked for rain, nor for it to stop, since the Spring of **1980**.

"I Would Like to See a Streak Of Lightning"

I have always liked to watch the lightning. About 8:30 one evening I could see the flashing of lightning and hear the thunder off in the distance towards the west. I went outside about 9:00 o'clock to see the streaks of lightning. The flash is pretty, but I like the streaks. I stood and watched for over an hour, but the storm never came my way. Overhead the sky was clear, I could see the stars, yet could see the flashes and hear the thunder rumble as well.

Looking up through the opening in the trees my driveway had made I said, "Lord, I would like to see a streak of lightning." It may have been ten seconds when a streak of lightning came across the opening from the east, it didn't come down just straight across the sky. There were no clouds toward the east, only toward the west. I waited for some time and saw no more streaks. Then I asked again and within ten seconds came another streak from the east, in the same place and fashion, a single streak almost straight. I repeated this several times and the only time I saw the streak was ten seconds after I asked and from the same place.

It was about eleven when I said, "Lord, I have to go in and get some sleep now; but I would like to see one really pretty streak before I go." Again, within ten seconds a streak came just as the others almost straight across the sky. I thought, Lord, I wanted a real pretty one, at that instant the streak blew up like a roman candle, at least six streaks spreading out from the original and then other streaks came from these, mixing and intertwining with each other. I said once again, "Thank you, Father."

"Stormy Wind Fulfilling His Word" (Psalm 148:8)

Again, it was 8:30 to 9:00 in the evening. I could see the flashes of lightning from my window which faced the south. I went outside and sat on a rock next to my flagpole and watched as three storms began to intensify.

One was toward the east southeast, one towards the south and one toward the west southwest. The seemed to flash in a sequence most of the time and I could be looking at the one that would flash next. It was awe inspiring.

As I watched they were getting closer and I wondered what it would be like for all three to come together, what a display. I sat and watched for some time. Then I said, "Lord I would like to see the sky filled with lightning" then I waited. They got closer to me, seemingly going to meet right over me. I saw very few streaks got to the ground, mostly the display was in the clouds. The closer they came the more beautiful the display. I waited. Several times I started to get up and go in, the rock was very hard, I was tired from a long day's work and needed sleep for tomorrow. Something inside said "Wait." I waited. The three came together and the display was very beautiful, but the sky was not filled, and I said, "Lord, that was real pretty, but the sky was not filled with lightning," I waited. The storms came closer, the activity increased as they got closer together. Then all these seemed to clash at the same time and there were well over a hundred streaks flashing across the sky at once. They were crisscrossing and flashing on off, on off, on off, rapidly. The fields were like daylight.

But in the unforgettable display there was an area, mainly to the south that was without any streaks. It wasn't a very big area, just a hole in the tapestry I had just witnessed. Again, I said "Lord, that was beautiful but there was a hole right over there that didn't have any streaks in it," I even pointed to it, then waited.

The lightning at this time was almost continuous, jumping from one side to the other and back. It wasn't very long before they all came on together. The way I was sitting, my back was toward the woods, and I could see a long way off to the east, south and west, so when the lights came on I could see a large portion of the sky. There were streaks of lightning as far as I could see east, south and west. The more it streaked the more streaks it generated until the whole sky visible to me was filled with lightning, not enlightened by flashes but by streaks. There were, I would estimate, three hundred or more going from horizon to horizon, crisscrossing and continuing to streak in every direction. No fireworks display could ever match the display of the awesome power of our Father to speak to the lightning and it will obey Him. I feel, it was just for me. It didn't matter to Him if it was one streak at a time or the untold number that I witnessed that night.

It only took a word, just a word. Only He, The Almighty, can send the lightning and it will say to Him, "Here we are!" Just like the Psalmist wrote, "Fire and hail, snow and vapors; stormy wind fulfilling His word" (Ps 148:8 KJV).

What the Father did in these two experiences was not, in any way, to say that I was of such upstanding character that He was obligated to do what I asked. It was just another God thing.

The Great Judgment of God

In **1982** I had the opportunity to go to Vermont. My boss owned 2800 acres just outside of Montpelier and a caretaker lived in the only house on the property. I took a tent and canteen. My intention was to fast, pray and seek to know the Lord better. As I was reading the Bible, a dream I had, maybe a year before, came to my mind. It was just as fresh as when I saw it, and I asked, "Lord, what does this dream mean?"

I was in the dream, I could hear explosions and see the flashes, there were clouds of what looked like dust, gray in color. Yet it was raining, not regular rain, the drops were long like streaks, maybe two feet, and it didn't get anything wet. There were people caught in the rain. There were no buildings, trees or grass, no place for them to get out of it. The flesh looked like it was melting off them, they were a gray color, and nothing but sagging skin and bone. Their eyes were just holes in the skull, just black holes, and the face was long and without the features of a normal face. The mouth was a gaping hole where lips had been.

Then I heard someone singing very jubilantly in a language I couldn't understand. Then a figure came into view from the left side, and it was me. I was singing and leaping and dancing and praising God in the midst of all the destruction.

I thought this must be the great judgment of God and wondered, what am I doing here? I continued to sing and dance, waving my arms and kicking my feet in wild abandonment

Then, as the dream was again so fresh in my mind, a verse of Scripture came to my mind and I looked it up, then another, and another. I turned to and read each one and knew what I had seen was the great judgment of the Almighty being poured out on mankind, but I was supposed to have been taken out before all this happened. Then another Scripture came to mind, I turned to it and read it. Then a voice inside me said, "*If it's not the way the church says it will be, don't be concerned, my Spirit is still with you.*"

We all mean well when we describe how it will be on that great judgement day, but only the Father really knows. The task given to the church is to tell about Jesus and what He has done to keep us, regardless of the circumstances we go through. The Scripture says, "The inheritance is laid up for them who are kept by the power of God."

It Must Have Started Right Over My Tent

I was reading and thinking on the Word one afternoon when I heard the wind blowing really hard. The tent wasn't shaking at all. I looked at the entrance to the tent and not a tree was moving, I looked out the back window and still the trees were not moving but I could still hear the wind blowing really hard. I looked out the entrance again. Just then the trees closest to the tent began to swing and twist and were swaying back and forth. Then the wind moved straight away from the tent, a strip of trees about 50 feet wide and 150 feet long were swinging and twisting violently, and the wind was really loud, then as suddenly as it started it stopped. The canopy of trees all around me were all of the same height, which consisted of several hundred acres, none of which were moving at all except the 50 by 150-foot strip. It must have started right over my tent.

A Vision Of Angels

One night as I lay in my tent thinking and praying, I saw, I suppose, a vision of angels. They were thin but tall. They were lined up on both sides of me as I lay there, and one stood at my feet. I saw none at my head. Their garments went to the ground, and they were pressed against each other so as to form a wall that I could not see through, except at my feet where only one angel stood. They didn't say anything, just watched for a while, then they were gone. Their faces all seemed so solemn, calm, as if watching a little baby.

The Mountain Of Blessing

I was reading and thinking on the Word when I heard a sound I had never heard before. I looked out the entrance and saw a large bird. I could tell it was some kind of woodpecker by the way it landed on trees and pecked, but I had never seen one so big. After returning home we looked in a bird book and found out it was a Phileated woodpecker. About a year later I had gone for a walk in the woods at home and laid down to rest and think. I heard a thump, thump, thump and opened my eyes without moving. In the tree about 6 feet from me was a Phileated woodpecker. I had not even heard of them in our area before but have seen plenty of them since. I believe this was the Father's way of taking me back to the Mountain of Blessing.

"I Climbed up the Mountain with Jesus"

When it came time to leave the mountain to go home, I didn't want to go. I got on my knees with my face on the ground and begged the Father to let me stay. The answer was no, and I started down the mountain.

Just a few months after getting home we visited a church on a Sunday evening. A lady asked the pastor if she could read a poem. The poem she read was titled "From Blessing to Service," by Virdie Gonoway.

It described how it was with me, as the first line of the poem states," I climbed up the mountain with Jesus-Away from my burden and care." It told of the blessings and the deep longing and desire to stay on the mountain with Jesus and of the knowledge He is with me wherever I go.

After the service I asked her if she would give me a copy of it, and she did. I had told very few people some of the things I had experienced on the mountain and when I read the poem, they thought I had written it; but my Father had prepared someone I didn't know to write it. Someone whom I had not heard of before its being read in church, by a lady who had never done anything like that before. As of the time of this writing, I still carry it in my Bible. The same one I went on the mountain with 29 years ago the end of this month.

Obedience to the Father is Never a Small Thing

In the first week of August after returning from Vermont, I was loading steel pipes for a drainage job we were doing and delivering them ahead of the equipment operators. The temperature was 110 degrees that day and I stopped at a roadside stand and got a Pepsi from the machine. The drink was so cold, water was dripping off it as soon as it hit the heat. I popped the top and drank half of it. Then I held it in front of me and said, "Now that's really good!" Then I heard someone say from behind me, "*Buddy, you don't need any more of those.*" I looked around and no one was there. The voice was out loud, not an inside voice. I said, "Right," and poured the rest out and have not drunk sodas since that day. When I looked back, I saw I had been drinking too many Pepsis. It was seemingly a small thing, but obedience to the Father is never a small thing; neither is disobedience.

Lord, Give Her My Blessing

I talked about earlier when my hip had been operated on, and as I said my Father's plan was at work. Although the operation was a success, as far as being able to walk and work again, the pain never went away. It was always there--sometimes more, sometimes less. There were times, and many of them, that I would wrap elastic bandages, two or three at a time around my hip to ease the pain and hold things tight. As years passed the hip grew worse and began to slip out of place. When it did, I would step on my right foot, stretch and twist and slip it back in. Sometimes I would be sleeping, and it would come out. Sometimes working the garden, that's when I stopped gardening. If you walked next to me when it was quiet you could hear my hip sliding in an out of socket. It was a sucking and then a squish as it went back when I put the weight on that leg. The lift on my shoe had now gotten to 1 ¾". I didn't know at the time that my thigh bone, the femur, was wearing into the hip bone. It got to the place at times I couldn't carry on a conversation because of the pain. When I got out of my truck I would have to hold onto the top of the door and pull myself up straight before I could begin to walk. When I got off the machine, I would have to do the same thing to be able to walk to the truck. It was a combination of my back and hip that brought on this condition.

During the same time, I had double vision in one eye. The eye doctor said the cornea was orange peeled. He didn't know what caused it and wanted to watch it for any changes.

One Sunday evening I visited a church that was having special meetings and the minister asked for people to come forward for a healing. I started to get up when I saw two ladies going forward, one helping the other to walk. I sat down and said, "Lord, give her my blessing, I'll stay like I am." Since then, I've learned that the Lord is not short on healing ability nor on the number He can heal. The lady did walk haltingly across the room by herself after being prayed for. I never saw her again, so I don't know the end of her story.

Double Portion

Monday evening after work I was sitting in my easy chair waiting for supper, the pain never stopping, only easing up at times, I got up and my legs gave way and I landed on both knees. At that instant my back pain left, I got up with ease. My Father gave me a healing even without a special prayer.

Next day I had an appointment with the eye doctor. When he looked at my eye through his instrument he rolled back in his chair, spread his arms and said, "Its gone! I don't know what caused it and I don't know what healed it." I told him I did. It was the Lord. He had no answer for that. I thought I was giving away my blessing, but I got a double portion.

The Father's Touch

My hip continued to pain me, intensifying at times. I would ask the Lord to ease the pain so I could hear what was being said. I'm not by any means saying my pain was the worst pain anyone could suffer. I'm just stating how it was with me.

A church in Preston had a visiting evangelist, C. R. Collins. I had never heard of him but knew the pastor, so I went to the meetings.

On Tuesday evening the pain was very intense, and I finally got into a position where it eased up enough for me to hear what Reverend Collins was speaking on. I sat as still as I could so as not to get the pain started again, and I heard the message, "Behold the Lamb of God." As I listened intently, I looked up away from the minister and saw a vision of Jesus, dressed in royal robes of many colors, coming closer and closer. There were clouds all around Him. He said nothing, only motioning to me and pointing to Himself--and the vision was gone. That was **1979**, and it is as clear today as it was the evening when I saw it. I cannot relate this story without tears and seeing again the vision in my mind.

Thursday evening, I returned to the meetings, the evangelist was just beginning to speak, maybe 10 minutes into the message when he stopped and said, "Someone here is lame, and I want you to come up and be prayed for." Another man had come to the meetings walking with a cane, so I waited. The evangelist spoke about 5 minutes more then stopped and said, "Someone in here is lame, God wants to heal them, please come forward." I went to the other man, asked if he were lame. He said, "I don't know about you, but I'm not." I said, "Well I am."

I walked up to the evangelist, he didn't ask anything, and his prayer didn't last but a few seconds, 20 maybe. I turned and walked back to the pew; but as I walked my hip and leg began to tingle. Then they began to get very warm. By the time I got to my seat, the pain was gone. I turned into the pew and remained standing.

In a little while the evangelist asked if I had something to say, I said, "Yes," then went on to say, "For the first time in 20 years I have not had pain in my hip." Until my mind goes, I will not forget these two events. I went on to tell of the warmth and tingling. The warmth and tingling lasted about two weeks.

The next day at work I had to drive an excavator about a mile and a half down a woodsy road, then walk back to my truck. Just one day before, walking 100 feet would give me intense pain. That Friday, the first day after the Father's touch, I walked about a mile and a half and when I got to the truck it didn't feel as if I had walked ten feet. As I write this, I could see myself walking briskly up the road, see me getting closer to the truck, opening the door and hopping in. I hopped in the truck without even a twinge of pain, which before I would have to raise my leg with my hand. After even a short walk, I would stop along the road to kick a can off it just because I could. I kicked the football for my sons; something I had never done. I even raced them and won, which before I couldn't run a lick.

I never saw or heard of Reverend C. R. Collins again. All of this was in my Father's plan. I would never have experienced such a touch from my Father, if I had not first had the 20 years before. It was worth it!

I had once put a shotgun to my hip and had my thumb on the trigger. I thought if I blew off my hip it would have to feel better than it did. But by my Father's mercy, He taught me. All this was in my Father's plan for me. Thank you, Father!

Relationship or Fellowship?

One night I laid in bed and repeated over and over the same phrase, "Lord, I want a better relationship with you." For over 2 hours I kept saying the same thing.

Then I had to go to the bathroom. I swung my feet off the bed and stood up. That's when a voice inside me said, *"Buddy, you can't have a better relationship with me than you already have."* I sat back down, my mind was racing, wow I thought, then the voice continued, *"You are related to me because of what my Son has done, and that cannot be improved upon, but you can improve your fellowship with me."* I wrote down the words so I wouldn't forget. The next morning, I looked up the words in the dictionary and learned that there is a big difference between the two. Webster's unabridged dictionary: Relationship – related by blood or marriage. Fellowship – intimate familiarity.

We can be related to someone and be alienated from them. I have cousins I have not seen in 30 years or more. We can only have fellowship when we are together. There is no way to have intimate familiarity unless we share a lot of time together.

"My Word, Driven by my Spirit"

When I was more able to move around in the woods, I would try to spend two or three hours alone walking. I didn't get in a hurry, just eased along talking and trying to listen to the Lord. I usually did more talking than listening.

One Saturday it was raining very hard, the wind was out of the northeast and very hard. I had walked about a mile through the woods, then along the edge of another woods which was blocking the fierceness of the wind. I came to the corner where the woods stopped, and a field began, and I leaned against a pine tree that was big enough to block the wind and rain for a while before I moved on. As I stood there, I watched the rain coming down in great sheets being driven by the very hard wind, gusting even higher at times. The rain was being blown at about a 20-degree angle and, when it gusted, the rain seemed to be a Great Wall moving across the open area.

As I leaned against the tree, I noticed the bark on my side was completely wet. The wind had made such a swirl as to wet the whole tree. As I looked, I saw water dripping off the rough bark of the pine tree. Looking under the edge I saw that it was still dry. I look around the other side where the wind was hitting, and, under the edge, it was wet. The rain was hitting with such force it was splashing up under the bark.

I looked at each side several times and then back to the open field in time to see a white wall of water being driven by the high winds. As I thought on what I had seen and was seeing, that inside voice said, "*It is my word driven by my Spirit that reaches the deepest crevices of a man's heart.*" I have said this before in this writing, but it is true. The sight is as fresh today as the day it happened, 25 to 30 years ago.

Hanging by a Thread

In the same area, late in the winter, it was a very mild day with only an occasional breeze. I had reached the corner of the wood and turned to go back. As I walked my eyes searched the field, sky and the woods edge, hoping to see some wildlife. Then I saw movement in a small tree in the hedgerow about 800 feet ahead.

I kept going at my slow pace, still scanning everything but focusing on the movement that would almost stop then start again but staying in the same place. When I got close enough, I saw it was a leaf of an oak tree that didn't lose its leaves until the new buds pushed them off. It was held on by a single thread. I passed the edge of the woods, and I was alongside the hedge row. I saw what was making the leaf spin fast, then almost stop, and spin fast again.

There was almost a nonexistent breeze that picked up then died down in almost a rhythmic manner. I notice some bushes near that were responding as well. The leaf never stopped, only slowed till it was barely moving. When it began to speed up, I would feel the breeze, then a laurel would begin to move. Finally, a holly bush began to shake as the breeze picked up a little more.

As the breeze slacked off, the holly would stop, then the laurel, then the leaf slowed but never stopped. I watched this several times, maybe 20 to 30 times, then the inside voice said, "*He that is least attached to the world is easiest move by my Spirit.*"

Years later I was able to take a picture of two leaves hanging side by side only by a thread on an otherwise green tree. I've seen many thread-hangers since then and said, "Lord , I want to be like that leaf. Holy Spirit move upon me as the wind moves the trees whichever way it will."

As I watched the leaves that were side-by-side, each hanging by a thread, I noticed that at some time one leaf would spin one way and the other the opposite way. Sometimes both would turn in the same direction, yet it was the same wind.

It wasn't a voice like so many times, only a thought implanted by the Father. Just because two people are going in different directions and doing things in different ways doesn't mean they are not of the Father and under the Spirit's direction. A lesson I have to repeatedly be refreshed on. I am not the one who directs, He is! My calling is to follow.

"Thanks for Spending Time with Me"

One Saturday I went for my walk with nothing specific on my mind. I had walked about 1000 feet into the woods when I came across a tree that had fallen. When it fell it had pulled some smaller trees down with it. They were now grown to, if standing straight, about 20 feet. The tops had been held down by the fallen tree which was lying about two feet off the ground. One end of the fallen tree was on the ground and the other was being held up by its limbs another smaller trees.

I said earlier if they were standing straight. Time under the other tree had bent them to form a roof over the fallen tree. It looked like a small Chapel. I went in and laid down on the fallen tree and just looked around a few minutes. It was surprisingly comfortable. Sensing the Presence of the Father I said, "Father, I'm here if you want to talk to me talk, if you don't then don't." I made a great effort to keep my mind from wandering and repeatedly brought it back to just waiting and listening, waiting to hear the still small voice of the Father.

After two hours or so I needed to return to the duties of the day. I had heard nothing, inward or outward, nor had any extra sense of His Presence. I said, "Lord, I need to go now," and began to walk towards the house. I had gone about 10 feet when it felt as if someone that was walking alongside me had put their arm around me and pulled me tight against them. I could feel the pressure on both sides, and a voice from inside said, "*Thanks for spending some time with me.*" We get lost in the busyness of life, even Christian things, when the Father wants us to spend some time with Him. To lay under a Tabernacle in the woods or sit by a stream, pond, or the ocean, to watch a sunrise or sunset, to be still and know that the Lord,

He is God, the Almighty, the Everlasting Father, the Savior of the world.

"Old Men will Dream Dreams"

About a year and a half, maybe two years, ago I had a dream, it was one of those that seemed like it was really happening. My grandson and I were standing 20 or 30 feet apart, there were some buildings one to my right and one in front of me. Lying on the ground between me and the building to my right was a steel H-beam about 20 or more feet long and 10 to 12 inches square.

There came a breeze and then a whirlwind. The whirlwind was column shaped, straight sided, and about 10 feet wide and 30 feet tall. It moved around picking up some dirt and debris, then moved over the steel H beam and moved it as if it were nothing.

It sat the beam down and came towards me, I stood still as it moved upon me. Once in the center all my clothing was stripped off. I was about 40 feet off the ground and saw my grandson on the ground, looking up. I threw the phone to him and said I wouldn't be needing it anymore.

My arms were folded across my chest, legs together as if laying down but was in upright position. The whirlwind took me up moving toward the building to my right. It was so gentle as it raised me, I barely missed the top of the building. I was thinking, "higher, take me higher." I went up over a large lake with trees all around it except where I had been. It was also gentle, and the view was unbelievable. I wanted to keep going but I began to return to the ground on the far side of the lake. It looked like nothing, but trees and I was coming down fast. When I got near the ground I saw a narrow stream, more like a dug channel, going straight through the woods. I was about three feet above the channel sitting in a laid-back position, feet forward going increasingly faster, yet all was peaceful.

At the end of the channel was a very old building, like an old feed-hardware store And I slowed down and glided into it. It seemed like I had seen it all before, very thick dust, cobwebs everywhere. I looked out the door and an old truck was coming, they stopped. I told them I needed some clothes, and they said they would send some. Soon an old car came and put a bag of clothes in the door for me. After dressing, they took me to a place that looked like a small almost derelict house with nothing but barren land around it. The people all came together, and I began to tell them about Jesus. It seemed they had called for me or someone to tell them what they needed.

When I began writing this dream I intended to only go to the tremendous view when I was very high over the lake, but I seem prodded to relate the whole story. As I see it now, I went from the comfort of my normal surroundings, to the height and gentleness of being without a care in such beautiful views of lake and woods and nothing of the old surroundings, back to the high-speed trip in tight quarters, then the slowing and stopping in an old but familiar building, to the sharing the gospel with a people I had never seen before, in a place I had never been. In each step of the way the peace of the whirlwind never left me nor was any fear experienced.

The next morning, when I awoke, I told my wife about the whirlwind and the peace I had felt. I wanted to go back to the whirlwind. I told her, if that is what a person feels after a hit on crack cocaine, I can understand why they are addicted after the first hit. I would ask the Lord to take me back to the whirlwind every night for several days, maybe weeks, then another very real dream came.

Whether by Whirlwind or Wheelchair

I was in a room, I thought, by myself. I was in a wheelchair, but it only had small wheels. The chair reclined and the person in the chair had to be pushed by someone else. I was close to a door and facing it. I could not move my arms, hands, legs or head. I could move my eyes and that was it.

My chair moved abruptly as if the feet were fastened in place and the head was making an arc. A woman carrying a basket had pushed me so she could use the door. She tried to open the door while holding the basket, but my chair came back and knock on the door closing the door before she could get through it. Again, this time with her foot, she pushed the chair a little harder. She grabbed the door, again, before she could get through it, my chair came back hitting it. This was repeated several times. About the third or fourth time, as I swung in an arc, I saw other people in the same kind of chair, all were helpless to do anything for themselves. There seemed to be, maybe, eight others.

Finally, she shoved the chair so hard it hit the wall hard and bounced away turning towards the others so I could see them, and she made it through the door. All we could do was move our eyes as we looked at each other. Then I began to sing, "Soon and very soon, we are going to see the King." After the first line I started again, singing the same thing. This time one of the others sang with me, then another and another, until we were all singing as well and as enthusiastically as we could, believing every word we sang.

The next morning, I relived the dream in my mind, the peace and comfort I felt although I had been kicked around and was totally helpless. I had nothing to complain about. Again, I told my wife of the great experience I had in the dream. That night I said, "Lord, it doesn't matter whether by whirlwind or wheelchair, take me back to the peace that passes all understanding that only You can give. I am content in whatever state my Father chooses for me. Pain or pleasure is all the same when it's Your perfect will."

During a Prayer Ride

During a prayer ride with some others, I had closed my eyes as the others prayed according to the Spirit's leading. When they had finished there was a pause. I began to see, what I will call a vision.

I saw the Lord, part of His face, only one eye. It looked sad then closed. I saw a high, very high red brick wall. The yard was a beautiful green, very well maintained, and it ran all the way to the wall. There were no shrubbery or plants of any kind, just grass. The red bricks were very red, as if just cleaned, the mortar was a bright white.

At the top of the wall for very thick vines, so thick I could not see the top of the wall. There were no vines at the base of the wall. They were growing from the top down, beginning to cover the wall. The vines were growing from inside the walls, over the top and coming down to cover the outside.

It is not the external things, that we keep clean for the eyes to see, that choke the life out of us. It is the internal things we neglect in an effort to keep the outside looking good. "Who shall ascend into the hill of the Lord? Or who shall stand in His holy place? He that hath clean hands, and a pure heart;" (KJV Ps. 24:3, 4a)

Look into my Eyes… I Began To Feel His Aloneness

While on another prayer ride there were several of us together. While we were praying, with my eyes closed, I saw one of them behind a wall. It was narrow and up to his eyes. What facial features I could see were dark gray, the eyes were very sad and fearful. I told him it wasn't far around the wall, and he could be free. The foundation of the wall was so that if he pushed it, it would fall; yet pushed from the other side it was well braced.

Later, at another prayer time at a church, not a church service, just a few of us pastors were together. I asked this man to look into my eyes. He could not maintain a gaze. He would look, then turn away. During this short time of contact, I began to feel his aloneness, the fear of exposure, anxiety, the pain of his soul. I began to cry as I hugged him, my heart went out to him in his aloneness, even with others around.

I will not go into detail but several years later, his dark secret was exposed, not by him, but by someone who knew him intimately. The exposure brought no repentance, only denial of wrongdoing. As of this writing, I have not heard of any confession of guilt. My prayer is that it will come. The Word says, if we confess and forsake, we'll have mercy (Prov 28:13; John 1:9).

Almost, but Lost!

While doing drainage work, a dozer operator and myself were about 400 feet apart. We had worked together often and would keep an eye on each other in case of a problem.

As I would look at him, I began to feel what he was feeling. I continued to work a little while, each time I looked at him, a feeling of anxiety, frustration and anger would come on me. It seemed I could hear him talking with all these emotions and I could feel the inward pain. As I am writing this, I see him as if it had happened today. I feel that hurt and pain that I felt over 30 years ago. My eyes are wet with tears as the remembrance of that day is replayed in my mind. I shut my machine down and went to him and stopped him. I asked if he was OK or would he like to talk. He poured out all the emotions I had felt. He became calm afterwards; his problems were still there but he had peace now.

Several years before this, I had talked to this man about Jesus and salvation, tears ran down his face dripping off his chin. He said he would accept Christ on his way home. The next day as we checked over our equipment he said, "about last night, I decided to try a little longer on my own."

Though we talked about the Lord, conviction never came as it did that day. We would ride back and forth to work together. We were a team, when it came to work. I never heard from his inner man again. It was if something had died.

We finished that job; I went one way, and he went another. I had not seen him or heard from him in many years. One day I received a call from his son. He told me his dad had moved someplace down South a few years before and had had a stroke. His dad didn't think he was recovering fast enough, went for a walk in the woods, and killed himself. He was buried before his son knew he was dead. Sad, sad! Almost, but lost. Rejection of God's peace leads to the ultimate despair.

"Remember Lot's wife"

There was a young man, a bit on the wild side, he was churched but mainly because of the girls in church. He was driving fast and reckless, rounding a curve he hit the shoulder of the road, overcorrected and lost all control of the car. The car crashed back over the road, flipped and was totaled.

I was told that he would be in the hospital for three months because of the injuries: broken pelvis, hips and legs. A man that knew him asked me to go with him to see the boy. We went on a Tuesday. His mother and stepfather were there. We talked awhile and then prayed. We joined hands as we prayed. While praying it felt like the floor began to shake, then increased as if the building was shaking. After the prayer and opening my eyes it was evident the others felt it also. The mother and stepfather were shaking all over and were very pale and crying.

As I said earlier, he was to be hospitalized for three months; but also was to be on crutches for six months following his release.

Thursday he was released from the hospital. Sunday, he came to church using one crutch. The following Sunday he was in church, not using any crutches or canes. For some time, he was regularly in church, singing with others as a group. Things were going well. I didn't hear from him for many years. He got off track, led away, led astray. One day a knock came on his door. He answered, stepping outside, and was killed, shot by a "friend." Sad ending to a great testimony.

A Body Slain and a Soul Saved

Another young man had been brought up by foster parents in a Christian home. When he was old enough, he went out on his own. His foster parents and I attended the same church. The older he became, the further away he went. He became a bartender in a local beer garden. I went to the place where he was working, it was during the day and the place wasn't busy. So, we had time to talk.

He recounted his younger years living with his foster parents and going to church and having made a profession of faith in Jesus. He said he hated what he was doing but didn't know anything else and he wished he could get out of that kind of life.

Shortly after that, at a Wednesday evening prayer meeting, his foster mother was very heavy hearted over him as she prayed. When she finished her prayer, I prayed this prayer, "Lord, remove him from that environment that his soul will be saved in the day of judgment." Friday night that young man was killed in a car wreck less than a mile from the church we attended.

I couldn't help but believe that our Father heard and answered our prayer. He took him out of that environment, that his soul would be saved. We don't know how God will answer our prayers, but if we ask for a fish, he will not give us a serpent.

Prayer for a Stranger, Who Turned Out to be a Neighbor

A friend had been taken to the hospital in serious condition. When I got there, he was still in the emergency room, which consisted of curtains around the area of each bed. He was awake and we talked awhile. As he was talking to me, his voice faded, and the heart monitor began beeping and the line became straight.

I stepped back out of the way while the staff worked on him. In a very short time, they had him stabilized and heart beating at a regular beat again. In the meantime, someone had been brought into the bed next to my friend, as I said, with only a curtain between us.

As we talked, we could also hear what was happening next to us. Someone said, "We've lost her." Then we heard a beating sound and someone saying, "come back, come back." Then the word, "clear." Then we heard the snap of electricity, then "clear" and the snap again. They had recovered her. Meanwhile we had joined hands and were praying for whoever it was.

In a few minutes we heard, "the copter is here." They started to take her and had gotten about 15 feet when someone said, "we've lost her!" Back to the room, the pounding, the calling out "come back, come back" map, the calling come back, the "clear" and the snap again. Three times hit with the paddles. In a few minutes we heard she stable period we were still praying.

Again they started for the medevac, about 50 feet we heard, "We've lost her!" Back again to the room with more of the same, again three times with the paddles. "She's back!" And then, "she's stable." This time they made it to the copter, while we were still praying for her and the hospital personnel.

The lady, as it turned out, lived about a half mile from me and I had seen her often jogging on the shoulder of the road. About a week later I saw her and stopped to see how she was doing. She said when she arrived at Shock Trauma, they examined her and could not find anything wrong. They kept her overnight and released her the next morning, with no idea what had happened.

After about 10 days in the hospital, my friend came home. We believe our Father had put us there so we could join in prayer for this lady.

Not Good Enough

Another lady I had known for many years had gotten cancer, the type that destroys the blood cells. When I found out, I went to see her. By that time, she had been given several blood transfusions, one about every 12 to 14 days and it didn't seem to be helping. She had been told they would do one more and if it didn't work, there was nothing else they could do.

When I arrived, they told me her blood count was 5 and she was scheduled to have the last transfusion on Thursday of that week. This was Tuesday. She said she didn't think her healing would be here but in heaven because she wasn't good enough.

After talking with her some, I asked her husband to stand across the room from her and asked her what she saw. She said, "I see Bill." I then stood between them and asked, "What do you see now?" She laughed and said, "I can only see you." I told her how when we are in Christ Jesus, the Father only sees Jesus, not our sin, nor our faults, because we are complete in Him.

On Thursday when the doctor took her blood count it was 95 and she didn't need a transfusion. Her pain had stopped, and shortly after they went to visit her brother in Arizona for a week and had such a good time that they stayed two weeks.

It must have been over a year that I found out she had no more blood transfusions and had taken nothing for pain as she hadn't had any. Some more time passed, I'm not sure how long, and I went to visit her. She said she was doing well but was getting tired of being an example for others, she just wanted to go home. The next time I heard anything about her, she had died and was buried. Her husband said she wanted him to call me but couldn't find my number.

A Shaking Finger, a Stronger Friendship

A lady I'll call Sally was in her 70s and was hospitalized with an infection. She had never been in the hospital before. She said she could not see why she was there. She helped other people who couldn't do for themselves. She would talk about her unseen guest. She didn't attend church very much; she was busy helping others. It was looking like she would not leave the hospital. She was asking why she couldn't get well. She had done so much good and always talked about her unseen guest. I told her that maybe the Father was giving her time to get to know him better, as she had been so busy with others.

When I came again, she shook her finger at me and said, "I'm so glad He has given me this time to get to know Him better." She never lamented again about being in the hospital. Every time I visited her, she would start the same way, shaking her finger, and declaring that she was glad he had given her the time to get to know him better. Her condition worsened. She had been in the hospital for months. I went to visit her, and her family was there. They said she had not responded to anyone, not even the nurses. When she heard my voice, she stirred and began shaking her finger and mumbling. I knew she was again thanking the Father for the time He had given her to get to know him better. She settled down for a while and then became restless. I felt the impress of the Holy Spirit now to speak. I said, out loud, not shouting but as I would in talking. "Spirit of 'Sally' I command you in the name of Jesus to be free. In less than two minutes she left this life to be with her now seen Friend.

Released by Satan, Received into Glory

I had gone to the Hospice House to visit a lady I'll call "Mary." The lady in charge said it would be a while before she passed and had told her family to go home and get some rest, and she would call them when her condition worsened. I talked with Mary for a while and could tell she was being agitated by something. She began seeing things and talking very fast.

I felt that she was being attacked spiritually and asked to pray. I said, "Satan, this woman is a child of God, and you have no power or authority over her. I command you in the name of Jesus to take your hands off her and leave her alone." The Hospice lady came in right then and said she had never seen anything like that before. And that she had called the family as Mary left this life in complete peace only moments after I had, in the name of Jesus, told Satan to leave her alone.

Pretending to be Asleep, but Listening

This lady I'll call Jean. She had a life-threatening illness at the hospital. Her daughter was told that nothing could be done to restore her health. The doctors advised not to put her on a ventilator as it would only make her condition worse and cause more suffering. The daughter threatened to sue them if they didn't, so they did. Several weeks went by and her condition worsened. If someone rubbed her arm the skin would come off. Jean and her oldest daughter had some differences over the years and Jean now would not respond to her at all but pretend to be asleep. She also did the same to me. I knew her time was short, and all that bitterness had to go before she did. One morning I went to see her and no one else was there. She pretended to be asleep, but I talked to her anyway. I talked about bitterness and unforgiveness and accepting responsibility for her part in the broken fellowship.

I could tell she was hearing me. Although her eyes were closed, I could see them move. Her lips began to quiver. Then I spoke to her spirit, "Spirit of Jean, if you don't repent and turn from your bitterness you're going to hell."

Her eyes opened, her lips began forming words, tears ran down her face and she raised both arms toward me. I bent and she hugged very tightly. I asked for peace to replace all the other stuff. The next day when I came to see her, her oldest daughter was there. She said when she came in her mother held her arms up, they hugged each other and kissed one another. The daughter told me later that was the first time in many years her mother had kissed her. Every time the daughter came after that, they hugged and kissed each other. She knew that her mother had made peace with God.

Jesus Never Fails

I just talked about "Jean," now I'm going to back up some and fill in a blank. Jean, also had other children. One of her sons died. I'll call him Richard. I was asked to do the service. I had never seen him before, and the family was very tightlipped; no one wanted to talk about him. I talked to the lady he was living with, and she only talked of the day of his death, which was very sudden. After the viewing on my way home I told my wife, this one will take a lot of prayer. The next morning was the day of the funeral. I was accustomed to rising early to read Scripture and pray. After that my thought went to the funeral. I could sense something, I put my pen and paper down and said to myself, "I'm going to get a drink," and stood up. Then a voice said, "Sit down and write." I did, and the Lord revealed to me this man's life.

It started when he around three years old until his death. The Lord revealed his emotions even as a child. How he responded to others, how he covered his innermost feelings with laughter and a smile. As he grew, he never had any real friends. He was in a crowd, but never let on. In reality he was calling for help but help never came. He was a loner. As I talked about his life some didn't seem to like it, but I could only speak what I was told. As I came to the time of his death, I said all his life family and friends had failed him. He was crying out, but no one heard. He had done some things that were viewed as shaming the family, which the Lord brought out at the service. I was not popular after that.

Then came the day of his death. His girlfriend told me what happened. He had gone to the bathroom, and she heard something fall, she went in he was on the floor talking crazy-like. I asked what he was saying. She said crazy things. As she began to tell me, it was as if she was quoting verses of Scripture concerning heaven. This was the second time someone near death had been given a vision of heaven. I know at that point he had met Jesus and they had reasoned together then. I finished the message by saying although family and friends had failed him, Jesus never fails.

At the gathering afterward at his mother's house, the people were talking about how I must have been a longtime close friend of Richard. They found it hard to believe that I had never met him or even seen him before the viewing. The Spirit of God knew him and told me all that I needed to know. His mother didn't care much for me after that; but, as in the other writing, it was taken care of. Jesus never fails!

Not Expected to Live through the Night

One of the men at church asked if I knew a guy, I'll call him "Jim Beam." I didn't. He said he was in ICU at Easton and not expected to live through the night. He asked if I would go see him and pray for him. I did. He was not aware of my being there and was elderly. I asked the Lord to do what was best for him. I knew He would anyway. The next day he was taken out of ICU and sent to a Nursing and Rehab Facility. I began visiting with him fairly regularly. He would do nothing for himself at first. But he had a really great attitude, talking about Jesus and God's love and care. After some time he was able to be gotten out of bed and could meet with others. His main topic was Jesus.

He got to where he could get out of bed by himself. At times his sister would take him for a ride, he started getting around on his own. He would visit with others who were not feeling well and shared God's love with them. He didn't complain and always gave praise to the Lord for what He would do. He lived over seven years there and was always pointing others to Jesus. When, as he said, his time was up, he was satisfied. I will always have many good memories of this faithful servant.

"Nothing Short of a Miracle!"

One Friday I received a call from the brother of a longtime friend, classmate and coworker. He said, (I'll call him Frank), "Frank was on his way out." He was in ICU and not responding to anyone. when I got there, I found out that Frank had been that way for two weeks and the doctor said he would not live through the night. Frank was not aware of anyone being there. He had tubes everywhere a tube could be put, on the ventilator, hooked to several IVs.

The doctor was talking to Frank's brother, saying after two weeks they need to take him off all the support machines. They went aside to do the paperwork and I went into Frank's room. I told the Lord I didn't know what to pray for and left it up to Him. I went home. I went back early the next morning. I went to the room Frank had been in, the lights were off, the bed was made and raised up. I turned to leave, when a nurse asked if I needed help. I told her I had come to see Frank and they didn't expect him to live through the night, so I guessed he had died. She said, "Oh no, he's down on the main floor!" She then gave me the room number.

When I came to the room, the door was open, and I saw him at the same time he saw me. He said he had been asking to see me. No one had told me. He was sitting up in bed eating scrambled eggs, fried potatoes, bacon and biscuits, with a glass of milk. It was nothing like the day before. He had no tubes, no IVs and was feeling great. The doctor came in and said, "Mr. Frank, we gave you the most powerful drugs we have for two weeks. We took you off everything and here you are today. This is nothing short of a miracle!" He made the statement three times.

When a 3-Year-Old Wants Prayer

When my third son was around three years old my mother was taking care of him. I was at the shop at my dad's house. My mother came out with my son. She said she had some water boiling on the stove and my son took hold of the handle to see and poured the water on his hand and he wanted me to pray for him. I asked if she had put anything on it. She said no, he wanted me to pray. His hand was red, and blisters were starting to rise. I took his hand between mine and prayed. "Lord, take away the hurt, the burn, and the pain." When I opened my hands, the redness was gone, the blisters were gone, and he had no pain. Only God could do that.

126 Years Old and Running 35 Mph

I had a dog named Lobo. He was a very good dog; he watched over the children while they were playing. He began to cough a lot, so I took him to the vet. The vet said he had heartworms and asked how old he was. I said, 12 years old (which is about 84 human years). He said that the medicine to kill the worms would kill him.

The Vet told me that for $10 he would give me the drug to euthanize him, or for $15 he would do it, himself. I told him I had to think about it. As I left and was walking to my truck I said, "Lord when my children are sick I pray for them." I stopped and put one hand under his jaw and the other on his head and prayed for his health. The coughing stopped. And he resumed running next to my truck as I went to work at 35 mph. He always stopped when we got to the woods, and I pulled away. The Vet had given him three months. He was almost 18 years old (126 human years) when he died. And until the time he died, he was still running next to my truck at 35 mph.

Even a Goldfish Matters to God!

My oldest daughter had a goldfish that had lived longer than most goldfish. She was very attached to this fish. I came home from work, and she was very upset. Her fish was upside down with blood coming out of it. I couldn't lay hands on the fish, but I prayed. When I got home the next day my daughter was beaming. She said when she had gotten up that morning the blood was gone, and the fish was right side up. He lived five to six years after that and died one night after all of us were in bed. Only God could do that.

Just Walk Across

A coworker and I were cleaning roots off a ditch bank. It consisted of walking the ditch we had dug and cutting any roots that would hinder the seeding of the bank. We came to a tributary we had to cross. It was too wide to jump across, so my coworker put his axe on the bottom and pushed it until he hit solid ground. It had sunk about a foot into the soft bottom. Then using the axe to hold him up, he jumped to the other side. When I went to follow him I stepped next to where his axe had sunk and stepped across the ditch without sinking in the soft bottom. He looked very suspicious and asked, "How did you do that?" I felt led inside me to just walk across the ditch, and I didn't sink or get muddy.

Just Follow

Another time, I was digging a ditch in a very wet and muddy area. The survey crew came to me, and they wanted to show me the plans that were in their truck. They had hip boots on and were walking in mud about to their knees.

They started for their truck with me following. I was last in line, the man in front of me was knee deep in mud, I was just in my work shoes. As we were walking the man was talking to me and turned to look at me. When he saw that I was on top of the ground with barely any mud on my shoes. He, knee deep in mud, asked "How do you do that?" It was plain to see something was different. Again, just follow.

Instead, He Gave Me Wisdom

I was placing rocks on a shoreline and needed to lay filter cloth on the bank after preparing it to the right grade. The wind was coming off the water and I couldn't get the filter cloth to go out far enough. Whatever I tried didn't work. I asked for the wind to stop, but it only blew harder.

I couldn't do the job without the filter cloth being in the right place. I tried, but nothing I did worked. Then an inward voice said, "lay the cloth on the ground and slide it out on the water." The water and the cloth sealed when it met the water. The wind couldn't get under it to blow it back. I used rocks to pin the cloth down and tossed them down the sides, then across the end and it was in place, and I finished the job. Instead of stopping the wind, He gave me wisdom that I learned to use at other times.

"Just Go Forward"

I was spreading material on the ditch bank using a dozer. I went into a stump hole filled with mud and the dozer wouldn't back out. The blade although raised high was almost completely under the mud. Usually when this happened, I would cut some logs and chain them to the tracks. Sometimes I would use short chunks, 2 1/2 foot to 3 feet, and chain one to each track. As I stood on the ground, I could lay my chain on the top of the dozer cab which was about elbow height to give an idea of how deep the machine was down in the mud.

I tried what I knew to do, it didn't work. An inside voice said, "just drive straight ahead." The angle of the dozer was still pointed down. I said, "it will only go deeper." I cut more chunks and logs. The voice said again, "just go straight." I said again it will only go deeper. I fixed my chains and tried my way again. When I had broken all my chains and was still stuck again, that voice said, "just go straight ahead." I started the engine, pulled the throttle back and put it in forward. The blade was up all the way, it went out of sight. I said, "see I told you it would only go deeper! Now what?" At that point, the track grabbed onto something, and the dozer went almost straight up, then flopped down on top of the ground completely out of the mud. I had to stop right then and say, "Lord I'm sorry, you know best in all things."

"There's No Way!"

On another job, clearing for a drainage ditch, it was very wet, soft ground and I was using a dozer. It was not a wide track machine, not adapted to that kind of ground. I was almost finished when the surveyor came. He said there was no way that dozer could clear that ground! But it was done and in less time than expected. Again, it was the Lord's instructions.

"I Saw It!"

The boss and I were on a farm going over a job. We had a crew clearing out roots in an adjacent field. They were using a backhoe to carry the roots to the disposal area. As the boss and I were talking, I was watching across the field. I could see the top of the backhoe which meant it was tilted at a very bad angle. I knew something was wrong. When I told the boss he said he would let me handle it, he was leaving.

When I got there the operator had run the backhoe over the slope of a ditch, with one front wheel was completely hanging in the air. The rear wheel, on the same side, was over the bank. We didn't have the equipment to pull it back up. I told them I would need to pray.

I started the backhoe, prayed for wisdom, and as the Lord said what to do, I did it. When I put the backhoe in gear, I throttled it up, swung the hoe attachment and dropped it. I caught it just before it hit the ground and hit the right brake. The machine pivoted on the rear wheels, with the front wheels hanging in the air over the ditch. I let off the brake, the front wheels still in the air, and backed the machine onto solid ground.

One of the men began jumping up and down, waving his arms frantically and shouting over and over. "I saw it, I saw it!" Then he explained, "a hook came down out of the sky and caught the backhoe, lifting it to the ground. And he said it again while still jumping and waving his arms. He was so adamant; I believe he saw something. However the Lord chooses to provide what we need, is okay with me.

Calming the Inner Storm

I was on my way to the hospital to visit some people. When I got to the light at Easton, I was in the lane to go straight into town but had to stop for the red light. A car came alongside me, I recognized the ones in it. They turned left, while I went straight.

When I went through the hospital doors to the front desk, those same people were there. The desk clerk asked where I was going. The people looked at me and said I was going with them. So I did. I didn't know that the lady's husband was in the hospital. When I came to him, he was rocking side to side and turn his head back and forth as far as he could, while moaning and making a chewing motion.

They said he had been like that for two days. He had not spoken anything. When I began to talk to him, his wife said he had started picking up the Bible but said he couldn't understand it. I began to tell him about Jesus and why he had to die for us. He stopped rocking and chewing and turning his head. He stopped moaning and just looked at me as I talked. I told him about salvation and repentance and faith toward God because of what Jesus had done on the cross. I told him that, even if he couldn't talk, God would hear his heart and his mind's prayer. I told him to share with the Lord his heart. The peace of God came on him. His family told me later that he never started the rocking, moaning and twisting again, but was calm until his death. Only God can calm the inner storm and give peace.

Recovered from the Gates of Hell!

A man I worked with was sick. He had been operated on for cancer. He was being fed by a tube in his stomach and breathed through a hole in his throat. To talk, he had to put his finger over the hole and force air through the vocal cords. His condition was worsening, and the nurse began coming daily to his home. She told the family that he couldn't live through the night.

The next day, after checking him, she said it again. His body was not accepting any of the food given him. This went on for two weeks. The family was exhausted. I visited on the Thursday evening before he died. While I was with him, his family went to sleep so I stayed until they woke up, which was near morning. Thursday evening, he was very agitated, and he was twisting and groaning. His face was all wrinkled as if in great pain. His daughter was on the bed on her knees trying to comfort him. I believed it to be a spiritual battle. I asked the Lord to rebuke Satan and his demons, and to deliver this man from the torments. In seconds, he was still with all the wrinkles gone! His face was as smooth as a young child.

His daughter said that if she had not seen it with her own eyes, she wouldn't have believed it. She said she was sure her father was going to hell; but, after seeing what the Lord did, she was sure the Lord had accepted and saved him. Only God can recover people from the gates of hell.

Mistaken for an Angel!

I was going home from work and was coming to an intersection of a major highway. I was a good way from the intersection, but the road was straight, and I could see the intersection ahead. As I looked at it, I began to feel different emotion. Anxiousness, frustration, some anger and fear. The closer I got, the more intense were my feelings. When I was close enough, I could see what was happening.

A young man in a pickup was trying to pull a car. A young lady was driving, and two small children were in the car. The young man would hook the chain, get in his pickup and start to pull away and then the chain would come loose. He would back up, hook up, and try again with the same results. This happened several times as I got closer to the intersection. When I got to the light and could crossover, I stopped. I asked if I could help, the young man refused, and said they could handle it.

I asked him to let me pull the car while he drove it and his wife could drive his pickup. Again, he said no. I told him the emotions I had felt. And said that his wife was afraid, anxious, and he was very frustrated at her. I asked each of them to confirm that these were their feelings. They both did. I said again, let me pull you and let your wife drive your pickup. He said he was going some distance. I said it doesn't matter, I'll take you wherever you're going. He moved his pickup, we hooked mine to the car and made the trip without any more problems. When we arrived, he unhooked my truck. I asked if they were alright, and they said yes. So, I left.

Sometime later I was at a viewing and a young couple asked if I remembered them. I didn't until they told me, they were the ones I had helped. They told the man behind them; this is the angel that helped them. They said Sunday they told in church how an angel had helped them. They said when they unhooked the truck they looked around and my truck was gone. They said it must have been an angel. I believe there was an angel that directed me to do what I did, the Angel of the Lord. I really can't tell you what it's like to be mistaken for an angel. Try it sometime!

The Fireball Was As Big As My Head

When I worked at a bakery, I had a few things that the Father took care of before asking. We had several pieces of equipment that ran on 220 volts and had to be plugged into an outlet. After a while, the plugs got worn. I had four of them explode in my hands. I will speak of only one of these times.

It was a roll slicer that had a cord hanging from the ceiling. It ended well above the equipment, and I had to get on something to reach it. There was a 55-gallon metal drum of mineral oil near, so I got on it to reach the cord. When I plugged it in, it exploded. It was heard over the whole plant, and they said the fireball was as big as my head. The fuse didn't blow, and sparks were shooting all around. I took hold of each wire, ran my hands to the plug and unplugged it. Both hands were out of sight in the fireball. But, I didn't get shocked, or burned. The hair on my hands were singed and the upper parts of my hands were black from the melting plastic. Only God prevented me from being electrocuted. The KJV Bible uses a word, "preventest" in Psalm 21:3. When I looked this word up it meant, "to prepare beforehand." He had already planned ahead for my actions!

I Heard a Crackling Sound

Another time I was operating the bread wrapper and had to replace the film we wrapped the bread in. In doing this I had to put my hand in the machine to push the paper through. When I did, I heard a crackling sound. I stopped and didn't move. Slowly, I looked in to see what the noise was. Electricity was jumping from my fingers to the metal plate below. I felt nothing. I saw the wire to the heater was sticking to the back of my hand. I lowered my hand to the metal plate and took it out. I turned the current off and had the wires re-attached to the heater. The heater was 220 volts, yet I felt nothing. Also prepared ahead of time. Before the world began, all of my members were written of, the Bible says.

270,000 Volts!

While operating heavy equipment, I was working near power lines, sometimes far nearer than I should have been. The hair on my body would straighten out. The sign read not to get within 15 feet of the lines. The ditch I was digging was directly under the wires and they were very low. I had the boom down as far as it would go and was about a foot away from the wires. The wires made a turn, and the ditch went straight, so I wasn't under any hazard. My Father had insulated me from the 270,000 volts in those lines, again already beforehand.

Preserved Yet Again

While digging next to a road ditch, I noticed something unusual. Wire was balling up on one side of the bucket. All underground wires were located, and the ditch was to be staked away from them. I stopped to see what was going on. The power cable was somehow in the ditch area. And I had scraped the grounding shield off the wire without cutting the wire. Already beforehand!

Seeing our Father through our Work

So many things have happened that cannot be attributed to anything but God's work. A lady was having problems getting a permit for us to do a job for her. I was asked to talk to the permitting agency. After the project was completed, I received a note and a book, "His Gifts to Me" by Marie Chapian. I am only partially reporting the note. "I can't thank you enough for handling the situation with aplomb. I truly believe that God's good work was shown to me through you on this project. It was becoming a nightmare to me, and you stepped in, with God's grace, and dispelled the fears from me, bringing the project to a satisfactory completion to all concerned." What more can we ask than for others to see our Father through our work. Jesus said, "if you have seen me, you have seen the Father also."

Lay Hands on it

I was at another church one evening. After the services, my family and I were in the car. The pastor went by in front of my car and said I had a headlight out. I got out and looked, it was. I said, "you know what the Bible says, lay hands on it." I put my hand on the fender over the light, the light came on. I never changed that light, and it never went out again.

Start the car!

One Sunday after church, a lady came back inside and said her car wouldn't start. I went out, asked her to try it, she did, and it didn't start. I asked her to open the hood. I put both hands on the fender and told her to start the car, I didn't say, try to start the car, I said, "start" the car. It started right away. She later said it always started after that and never needed any work done on it.

The Living God Sees All Things

I have many other "only God" times, but these are written that you may know the Living God is near every one of us, and you don't have to be someone of great importance for Our Father to see our need and respond, even ahead of time.

I'm going to tell of one more time at work. We were doing a bulkhead for shoreline retention. When we got to the corner, it was not a normal 90-degree angle. The last piece of sheeting had to be cut to fit just right. Sheeting is a 3" x 10" treated board with tongue and groove force-tight wall. It had to be cut full length at the exact angle we needed. The length of the board was 20 feet.

First, I measured to get the angle, then used a chalk line to mark the cut. When I had gotten the chainsaw to make the cut, I didn't feel right. I told my coworker that I wasn't comfortable and to turn the board over. In doing that, it put the chalk line on the bottom. He said, "you can't follow a chalk line when it's on the bottom." Although I couldn't physically see it, I felt very comfortable in cutting it that way.

When I finished the cut, we turned the board over and I had cut it so half of the chalk line was left. One area, about a foot long, the whole line was left and then went back to half the line. I had to step over the board that we had the sheeting on, and that move changed the angle of the saw. My "inside" felt the move and lined me back up so everything was correct. My coworker said that it was impossible for the measurement to be correct. But God knew otherwise. In being comfortable in my spirit, I knew all would be well, as I had experienced this so many times. It was perfect! He later told the boss what had happened, and it had to be God working in me. You can't cut what you cannot see. But our Father does see all things visible and invisible.

My Prayer for You

These stories are not the half of what has happened during my lifetime. God's hand and eye have been on me all the days of my life. I didn't come into this world knowing Jesus. But because of others who did, and the moving of the Holy Spirit, I came to know Him as Lord and Savior. And as my ever-present God. I know there is no other name given among men whereby we must be saved. My hope is that all who read this little book will come to know Jesus as their Savior, so there will be no end to the story of your life.